D1600929

STREET WEAR

THE ULTIMATE GUIDE TO STARTING YOUR OWN BRAND

BY CRAIG WASHINGTON

TABLE OF CONTENTS

Introduction 1

Chapter 1: Identifying Your Target Market 2

Chapter 2: Developing a Unique Brand Identity 3

Chapter 3: Designing and Producing Your Clothing 5

Chapter 4: Marketing and Selling Your Products 7

Chapter 5: Building a Strong Team 9

Chapter 6: Finding a Niche 11

Chapter 7: Finding a Manufacturer 13

Chapter 8: Finding People to Collaborate With 15

Chapter 9: How to Gain Publications 16

Chapter 10: Staying Ahead of the Curve 17

Chapter 11: The Importance of Having a Website for Your
Streetwear Brand 19

Chapter 12: Building a community 22

Chapter 13: The Importance of Hiring a Photographer and Taking
High-Quality Photos for Your Streetwear Brand 24

Chapter 14: Giving Back 27

Chapter 15: Never Give Up 29

Chapter 16: My Personal Experience Starting Top Notch NME.............. 31

Chapter 17: Advice for Other Streetwear Entrepreneurs......................... 32

Chapter 18: The Differences Between Screen Printing, DTG, and
Sublimation Cut and Sew 33

Chapter: 19: Pop Up Shops: A Powerful Marketing Strategy for
Your Brand.. 36

Chapter 20: Trademark and Copyright 43

Conclusion.. 49

Bonus Chapter... 50

Chapter 21: How to Do a Drop or Launch for a Product for Your
Streetwear Brand... 51

INTRODUCTION

S treetwear is a style of fashion that originated in the streets of urban areas. It is characterized by its casual, comfortable, and often rebellious nature. Streetwear has become increasingly popular in recent years, and there are now many successful streetwear brands on the market.

If you are interested in starting your streetwear brand, this book is for you. It will provide you with the essential information you need to get started, including:

- How to identify your target market
- How to develop a unique brand identity
- How to design and produce your clothing
- How to market and sell your products
- How to build a successful business

CHAPTER 1
IDENTIFYING YOUR TARGET MARKET

The first step in starting a streetwear brand is to identify your target market. Who are you trying to sell to? What are their needs and wants? Once you know who your target market is, you can start to develop a brand identity that appeals to them.

Here are some questions you can ask to help you identify your target market:

- What is the age range of your target market?
- What is the gender of your target market?
- What is the socioeconomic status of your target market?
- What are the interests of your target market?
- What are the needs and wants of your target market?

Once you have a good understanding of your target market, you can start to develop a brand identity that appeals to them.

CHAPTER 2
DEVELOPING A UNIQUE BRAND IDENTITY

Your brand identity is what will set your streetwear brand apart from the competition. It should be unique, memorable, and relevant to your target market. Your brand identity should be reflected in everything from your logo and website to your clothing designs and marketing materials.

Here are some tips for developing a unique brand identity:

- **Start with a strong concept.** What is the core message of your brand? What do you want your brand to stand for?
- **Choose a unique name and logo.** Your name and logo should be memorable and easy to pronounce. They should also be relevant to your target market and your brand identity.
- **Develop a strong visual identity.** Your website, social media pages, and marketing materials should all be consistent with your brand identity.
- **Tell your story.** What is the story behind your brand? Why did you start your business? What are your goals for your brand?

- Be consistent. Your brand identity should be consistent across all channels. This means using the same colors, fonts, and imagery on your website, social media pages, and marketing materials.

CHAPTER 3

DESIGNING AND PRODUCING YOUR CLOTHING

O nce you have developed a unique brand identity, it is time to start designing and producing your clothing. If you do not have any experience in fashion design, there are many resources available to help you get started. You can also hire a freelance designer to help you create your clothing line.

Here are some tips for designing and producing your clothing:

- **Start with a sketch.** Before you start sewing, it is an innovative idea to sketch out your designs. This will help you visualize the final product and make sure that everything is proportional.
- **Choose the right fabrics.** The fabric you choose will have a significant impact on the look and feel of your clothing. Make sure to choose fabrics that are comfortable and durable.
- **Get feedback from friends and family.** Once you have a few designs, show them to your friends and family for feedback. This will help you make sure that your designs are on the right track.

- **Find a manufacturer.** Once you have finalized your designs, you need to find a manufacturer to produce your clothing. There are many manufacturers out there, so it is important to do your research and find one that is reputable and has a good record of accomplishment. ("Gold IRA Rollover: The Ultimate Guide | Best Daily | collegian.psu.edu")

CHAPTER 4

MARKETING AND SELLING YOUR PRODUCTS

O nce you have your clothing line designed and produced, it is time to start marketing and selling your products. There are many ways to market your streetwear brand, including:

- **Social media:** social media is a wonderful way to connect with your target market and promote your brand. ("Connect with Your Startup's Target Market - Faster Capital") Make sure to create engaging content that will capture their attention. This could include photos of your products, behind-the-scenes footage, or even just funny or interesting posts. You can also use social media to run contests and giveaways, which can help you attract new customers.

- **E-commerce:** E-commerce is a convenient way for customers to buy your products online. Make sure to create a user-friendly website that is easy to navigate and checkout. You can also use e-commerce platforms to sell your products on other websites, such as Amazon and eBay.

- **Retail stores:** If you have the budget, you can also sell your products in retail stores. This can help you reach a wider audience and build brand awareness. When choosing retail stores, make sure to choose stores that are relevant to your target market.

- **Collaborations:** Collaborations are a great way to reach a new audience and promote your brand. You can collaborate with other streetwear brands, musicians, artists, or even athletes. When choosing collaborators, make sure to choose people who are relevant to your target market and who have a strong following.

- **Public relations:** Public relations can help you get your brand in front of the media and generate positive buzz. You can hire a PR firm to help you with this, or you can do it yourself by reaching out to journalists and bloggers.

- **Events:** Events are a great way to connect with your target market and promote your brand. You can host pop-up shops, fashion shows, or even just meet-and-greets. Events are a great way to get people excited about your brand and generate sales.

- **Word-of-mouth:** Word-of-mouth is one of the most powerful marketing tools there is. When your customers are happy with your products and service, they will tell their friends and family about it. Make sure to provide excellent customer service and go beyond for your customers.

By following these tips, you can market and sell your streetwear products and build a successful brand.

CHAPTER 5
BUILDING A STRONG TEAM

You cannot do everything yourself, so you will need to build a team of talented people to help you with your business. This team should include people with experience in marketing, sales, design, production, and accounting.

Sure, here are some more insights on building a team of talented people to help you with your business:

- **Start by defining your team's goals.** What do you want to achieve with your business? Once you know your goals, you can start to identify the skills and experience that you need on your team.
- **Be clear about your expectations.** When you are hiring new team members, be sure to set clear expectations for their roles and responsibilities. This will help to ensure that everyone is on the same page and working towards the same goals.
- **Create a positive work environment.** A positive work environment is essential for a successful team. Make sure that your team members feel valued and appreciated, and that they have the resources they need to do their jobs effectively.

- **Provide opportunities for growth and development.** Your team members are your greatest asset. Invest in their development by providing them with training and opportunities to develop their skills. This will help them to be more successful in their roles and contribute even more to your business.

Here are some additional things to keep in mind when building your team:

- **Diversity is key.** A diverse team brings a variety of perspectives and experiences to the table, which can lead to more creative and innovative solutions.
- **Look for people who are passionate about your business.** When people are passionate about what they do, they are more likely to be engaged and productive.
- **Create a culture of trust and respect.** A team that trusts and respects each other is more likely to be successful.
- **Celebrate successes.** When your team achieves a goal, take the time to celebrate their success. This will help to build morale and motivation.

Building a successful team takes time and effort, but it is worth it. A talented team can help you to achieve your business goals and grow your business.

CHAPTER 6
FINDING A NICHE

To be successful, you need to find a niche in the streetwear market. This means finding a specific group of people who are interested in your brand and what you have to offer.

Here are some detailed instructions on how to find a niche for your streetwear brand:

1. **Start by brainstorming a list of your interests and passions.** What are you passionate about? What do you know a lot about? What are you good at? Once you have a list of your interests, you can start to narrow it down to find a niche that is right for you.

2. **Do some research on the streetwear market.** What are the current trends? Who are the major players in the market? What are the needs and wants of your target market? Once you have a good understanding of the streetwear market, you can start to develop a niche that is unique and fills a need in the market.

3. **Be creative and think freely.** Don't be afraid to be different. The best way to find a niche is to produce something that no one else is doing.

4. **Don't be afraid to experiment.** The best way to find your niche is to experiment and try different things. Do not be afraid to fail. Failure is a part of the learning process.

5. **Get feedback from others.** Once you have a few ideas, get feedback from others. Ask your friends, family, and other people in the streetwear industry for their opinions. This feedback will help you refine your ideas and find a niche that is right for you.

Here are some additional tips for finding a niche for your streetwear brand:

- **Focus on a specific style.** Don't try to be everything to everyone. Instead, focus on a specific style or aesthetic. This will help you stand out from the competition.

- **Target a specific audience.** Who is your ideal customer? What are their needs and wants? Once you know your target audience, you can tailor your brand to appeal to them.

- **Be consistent.** Once you find a niche, stick with it. Do not try to change your brand too often. This will confuse your customers and make it harder for them to connect with your brand.

- **Be patient.** It takes time to build a successful streetwear brand. Do not expect to become an overnight success. Just keep working hard and eventually, you will achieve your goals.

CHAPTER 7

FINDING A MANUFACTURER

One of the most important steps in starting your streetwear brand is finding a manufacturer. The right manufacturer can help you bring your vision to life and produce high-quality products that your customers will love.

There are a few things to keep in mind when choosing a manufacturer:

- **Location:** Where is the manufacturer located? This will affect the cost of shipping and the time it takes to get your products.
- **Capabilities:** What types of products can the manufacturer produce? Make sure they have the capabilities to produce the items you want to sell.
- **Quality:** What is the quality of the manufacturer's products? Do some research to see what other people have said about their products.
- **Price:** What is the cost of the manufacturer's products? Make sure you are getting a fair price for the quality of the products.

Once you have found a few manufacturers that meet your criteria, it is time to start getting quotes. Be sure to get quotes for both the cost of the products and the cost of shipping.

Once you have received quotes from a few manufacturers, it is time to plan. Consider all the factors above when making your decision.

CHAPTER 8

FINDING PEOPLE TO COLLABORATE WITH

Collaborating with other people is a terrific way to grow your streetwear brand. By collaborating with other brands, artists, and musicians, you can reach a wider audience and expose your brand to new people.

There are a few things to keep in mind when looking for people to collaborate with:

- **Target audience:** Make sure the people you are collaborating with have a similar target audience to your own. This will help you reach more people who are interested in your brand.
- **Reach:** How many people do they reach? The more people they reach, the more potential customers you will be able to expose your brand to.
- **Credibility:** Are they credible in the streetwear community? If they are well-respected in the community, it will help you gain credibility with potential customers.

Once you have found a few people you would like to collaborate with, it is time to reach out to them. Be sure to explain your vision for the collaboration and why you think it would be a good fit for both of your brands.

CHAPTER 9
HOW TO GAIN PUBLICATIONS

Getting your brand featured in publications is a terrific way to reach a wider audience and build credibility. There are a few things you can do to increase your chances of getting published:

- **Build relationships with editors:** Get to know the editors of the publications you want to be featured in. Attend industry events, send them press releases, and reach out to them on social media.
- **Submit high-quality content:** When you submit content to publications, make sure it is high-quality and relevant to their audience. This will increase your chances of getting published.
- **Be persistent:** Don't give up if you do not get published right away. Keep submitting content and building relationships with editors. Eventually, you will start getting published.

CHAPTER 10
STAYING AHEAD OF THE CURVE

The streetwear market is constantly changing, so you need to stay ahead of the curve. This means keeping up with the latest trends and being able to adapt your brand to meet the needs of your target market.

- **Stay up to date on the latest trends.** The streetwear market is constantly changing, so it is important to stay up to date on the latest trends. You can do this by reading fashion magazines, following fashion blogs, and attending fashion shows.
- **Be creative and innovative.** Don't be afraid to be different. The best way to stay ahead of the curve is to produce something that no one else is doing.
- **Be willing to take risks.** If you want to stay ahead of the curve, you need to be willing to take risks. This could mean trying new things, expanding into new markets, or collaborating with other brands.
- **Be patient.** It takes time to build a successful streetwear brand. Do not expect to become an overnight success. Just keep working hard and eventually, you will achieve your goals.

- **Listen to your customers.** Pay attention to what your customers are saying and doing. This will help you understand what they want and need, and it will give you ideas for new products and services.
- **Be adaptable.** The streetwear market is constantly changing, so it is important to be adaptable. This means being willing to change your products, marketing, and even your brand identity if necessary.
- **Be prepared to fail.** Everyone fails at some point. The important thing is to learn from your failures and move on.

Have fun. If you are not having fun, it will be hard to stay motivated. So, make sure to enjoy the journey.

CHAPTER 11

THE IMPORTANCE OF HAVING A WEBSITE FOR YOUR STREETWEAR BRAND

I n today's digital age, it is more important than ever for businesses to have a strong online presence. If you are selling streetwear, a website is essential for reaching new customers and growing your business.

A website gives you a space to highlight your products, tell your brand story, and connect with potential customers. It is also a terrific way to drive traffic to your social media channels and generate sales.

If you do not have a website for your streetwear brand, now is the time to get one. Here are just a few of the benefits of having a website:

- **Increased brand awareness:** A website is a terrific way to introduce your brand to new customers. When people visit your website, they will learn about your products, your story, and your values. This can help you to build trust and credibility with potential customers.

- **Increased sales:** A website makes it easy for customers to shop for your products. They can browse your collection, read product reviews, and make purchases all from the comfort of their own homes.
- **Improved customer service:** A website gives you a way to provide customer service 24/7. Customers can contact you with questions or concerns about their orders, and you can respond to them quickly and easily.
- **Enhanced search engine visibility:** A website helps your brand rank higher in search engine results pages (SERPs). This means that more potential customers will be able to find your brand when they are searching for streetwear online.

If you are serious about selling streetwear, a website is an essential investment. It is a terrific way to reach new customers, grow your business, and improve your brand's online presence.

Here are some tips for creating a successful streetwear website:

- **Make sure your website is mobile-friendly:** More and more people are using their smartphones and tablets to shop online. Make sure your website is optimized for mobile devices so that customers can easily browse and purchase your products from anywhere.
- **Use high-quality images:** Images are one of the most essential elements of a streetwear website. Make sure your images are high-quality and visually appealing. This will help

to capture attention and encourage customers to shop for your collection.

- **Write clear and concise product descriptions:** Product descriptions are another crucial element of a streetwear website. Make sure your descriptions are clear and concise, and that they highlight the features and benefits of your products.
- **Offer free shipping and returns:** Free shipping and returns are a fantastic way to encourage customers to shop on your website. This will help to reduce the number of abandoned carts and increase sales.
- **Run regular promotions and discounts:** Running regular promotions and discounts is a terrific way to attract new customers and boost sales. You can offer discounts on individual products, or you can run site-wide sales.
- **Promote your website on social media:** social media is a terrific way to promote your website and reach new customers. Make sure you are active on social media and that you are sharing content that will resonate with your target audience.

By following these tips, you can create a successful streetwear website that will help you to grow your business.

CHAPTER 12
BUILDING A COMMUNITY

O ne of the best ways to build a successful streetwear brand is to build a community around your brand. This means creating a space where your customers can connect with your brand.

Here are some tips on building a community around your streetwear brand:

- **Create a strong online presence.** This means having a website, social media accounts, and even a blog. Make sure to post interesting and engaging content that will attract your target audience.
- **Host events.** This could be anything from pop-up shops to fashion shows. Events are a terrific way to get people excited about your brand and generate sales.
- **Partner with other brands.** This could be other streetwear brands, musicians, artists, or even athletes. When you partner with other brands, you can reach a wider audience and build brand awareness.
- **Run contests and giveaways.** This is a terrific way to generate excitement and engagement around your brand. Just make sure the prizes are something that your target audience would be interested in.

- **Be active on social media.** This means responding to comments and questions, running contests and giveaways, and sharing interesting and engaging content. When you are active on social media, you are more likely to connect with your target audience and build a community around your brand.
- **Be authentic.** People can spot a fake from a mile away. Be yourself and be genuine, and your community will appreciate it.

Be consistent. Don't just show up when you need something. Be present and engaged with your community regularly.

CHAPTER 13

THE IMPORTANCE OF HIRING A PHOTOGRAPHER AND TAKING HIGH-QUALITY PHOTOS FOR YOUR STREETWEAR BRAND

In today's digital age, visuals are more important than ever. When it comes to selling streetwear, high-quality photos are essential for attracting attention and generating sales.

A good photographer can capture the unique style and personality of your brand and help you to create images that will resonate with your target audience. They can also help you to create a consistent visual identity for your brand, which is important for building trust and recognition.

If you are serious about selling streetwear, it is worth investing in a professional photographer. A good photographer will be able to take photos that are both stylish and eye-catching, and they will help you to create a strong visual identity for your brand.

Here are some of the benefits of hiring a photographer for your streetwear brand:

- Professional photos will make your brand look more credible. When potential customers see high-quality photos of your products, they will be more likely to trust your brand and buy from you.

- Good photos will help you to stand out from the competition. In a crowded market, it is important to have photos that make your brand stand out from the rest. A good photographer can help you to create unique and eye-catching images that will help you to capture attention.
- High-quality photos will help you to increase sales. Studies have shown that customers are more likely to buy products when they see high-quality photos of them. If you want to increase sales, it is important to invest in good photos.

If you are looking for a photographer to shoot your streetwear brand, there are a few things you should keep in mind:

- Look for a photographer who has experience shooting streetwear. Not all photographers are created equal. When you are looking for a photographer to shoot your streetwear brand, it is important to find someone who has experience shooting this type of clothing. A good photographer will know how to capture the unique style and personality of your brand.
- Get a quote from multiple photographers before planning. Photographers charge different rates, so it is important to get a quote from multiple photographers before planning. This will help you to find the best photographer for your budget.

- Meet with the photographer in person before hiring them. Once you have found a few photographers that you are interested in working with, it is important to meet with them in person before hiring them. This will give you a chance to get to know them and see if they are a good fit for your brand.

Hiring a photographer is a terrific way to improve the visual appeal of your streetwear brand. By investing in good photos, you can make your brand look more credible, stand out from the competition, and increase sales.

CHAPTER 14
GIVING BACK

Giving back to the community is a terrific way to show your appreciation for the people who support your business. It can also help you to build goodwill and positive relationships with your customers, employees, and other stakeholders.

There are many ways to give back to the community. Here are a few ideas:

- Donate money or products to local charities. This is a terrific way to make a direct impact on the lives of those in need.
- Volunteer your time at a local soup kitchen, homeless shelter, or other organization that helps those in need. This is a terrific way to give back to your community and make a difference in the lives of others.
- Partner with a local charity or organization to raise awareness and funds for a cause that you care about. This is a terrific way to get your customers involved in giving back to the community.
- Host a fundraiser or event to benefit a local charity or organization. This is a terrific way to raise money and awareness for a cause that you care about.

- Offer discounts or promotions to customers who volunteer their time or donate to a local charity. This is a terrific way to encourage your customers to give back to the community.

No matter how you choose to give back, it is important to do something that you are passionate about. When you give back to the community, you are not only making a difference in the lives of others, but you are also making a difference in your own life.

Here are some of the benefits of giving back to the community:

- **It makes you feel good.** Helping others is a terrific way to boost your self-esteem and make you feel good about yourself.
- **It strengthens your relationships.** When you give back to the community, you are not only helping others, but you are also building relationships with people who share your values.
- **It makes your community a better place.** When you give back to your community, you are making it a better place for everyone.
- **It sets a good example for others.** When you give back to your community, you are setting a good example for others to follow.

If you are looking for a way to make a difference in the world, consider giving back to your community. It is a terrific way to make a positive impact on the lives of others and make yourself feel good at the same time.

CHAPTER 15
NEVER GIVE UP

Starting a business is arduous work, and there will be times when you want to give up. But if you are passionate about your brand, you need to keep going. Never give up on your dreams.

I know this from personal experience. When I first started Top Notch NME, I had a lot of challenges. I did not have any experience in fashion design or business, and I did not have a lot of money. But I was passionate about my brand, and I was determined to make it a success.

I worked hard, and I made a lot of mistakes along the way. But I never gave up. And eventually, my hard work paid off. Top Notch NME is now a successful streetwear brand with a loyal following of customers all over the world.

If I can do it, you can too. So never give up on your dreams. If you are passionate about something, go for it. Work hard, and never give up. And eventually, you will achieve your goals.

Here are some additional tips for never giving up on your dreams:

- **Stay focused on your goals.** It is easy to get sidetracked when you are starting a business. But it is important to stay focused on your goals and to keep moving forward.
- **Don't be afraid to ask for help.** There are a lot of people who are willing to help you succeed. Do not be afraid to ask for help from your friends, family, mentors, or other entrepreneurs.
- **Don't give up when things get tough.** There will be times when you want to give up. But it is important to keep going. Remember why you started your business in the first place and use that as motivation to keep going.
- **Celebrate your successes.** It is important to celebrate your successes along the way. This will help you stay motivated and keep moving forward.

CHAPTER 16

MY PERSONAL EXPERIENCE STARTING TOP NOTCH NME

I started Top Notch NME in 2017 to create high-quality, affordable streetwear that was both stylish and comfortable. I had always been passionate about fashion, and I wanted to create a brand that represented my unique style.

When I first started, I did not have any experience in fashion design or business. But I was determined to make my dream a reality. I started by sketching out my designs and then sewing them myself. I also started a blog to share my designs with the world.

Over time, my blog started to gain traction, and I began to build a following. I also started to sell my designs online and at local boutiques. In 2012, I was able to expand my business and focus on Top Notch NME full-time.

Since then, Top Notch NME has grown into a successful streetwear brand. We have a loyal following from customers all over the world, and our products have been featured in major magazines and publications.

I am so proud of what we have accomplished, and I am excited to see what the future holds for Top Notch NME.

CHAPTER 17
ADVICE FOR OTHER STREETWEAR ENTREPRENEURS

If you are thinking about starting your streetwear brand, here are a few pieces of advice:

- **Be passionate about your brand.** If you are not passionate about your brand, it will be hard to succeed.
- **Be yourself.** Do not try to be someone you are not. Your brand should reflect your unique style.
- **Don't give up.** Starting a business is challenging work, but it is also incredibly rewarding. Never give up on your dreams.

I hope these tips help you on your journey to starting your streetwear brand.

CHAPTER 18

THE DIFFERENCES BETWEEN SCREEN PRINTING, DTG, AND SUBLIMATION CUT AND SEW

When it comes to printing on garments, there are a few different methods that can be used. Each method has its own advantages and disadvantages, and the best choice for you will depend on your specific needs and budget.

In this chapter, I'll discuss the three most common methods of garment printing: screen printing, direct-to-garment (DTG) printing, and sublimation cut and sew. I'll explain how each method works, as well as its pros and cons.

Screen Printing

Screen printing is one of the oldest and most popular methods of garment printing. It's a versatile process that can be used to print on a variety of materials, including cotton, polyester, and nylon.

Screen printing works by using a mesh screen to transfer ink onto a garment. The ink is applied to the screen using a squeegee, and the excess ink is then removed. The process is repeated for each color that you want to print.

Screen printing is a relatively affordable method of garment printing, and it's well-suited for large-scale production. However, it can be time-consuming to set up the screens, and it's not as versatile as some of the other methods.

Direct-to-Garment (DTG) Printing

Direct-to-garment (DTG) printing is a newer method of garment printing that's quickly gaining popularity. It's a digital printing process that allows you to print directly onto garments without the need for screens.

DTG printing is a more versatile process than screen printing, and it can be used to print on a wider variety of materials. It's also a more precise process, and it can be used to print more complex designs.

However, DTG printing is more expensive than screen printing, and it's not as well-suited for large-scale production.

Sublimation Cut and Sew

Sublimation cut and sew is a process that combines two different methods of garment printing: sublimation and cut and sew.

Sublimation is a process that uses heat and pressure to transfer ink onto a substrate. In the case of sublimation cut and sew, the ink is transferred onto a sublimation-coated fabric.

The sublimation-coated fabric is then cut and sewn into a garment. This process allows you to create garments with high-quality prints that are also durable and long-lasting.

Sublimation cut and sew is the most expensive method of garment printing, but it's also the most versatile and durable. It's a great option for high-end streetwear brands and other businesses that need high-quality prints on their garments.

Choosing the Right Method

So, which method of garment printing is right for you? It depends on your specific needs and budget.

If you're looking for an affordable method of printing large quantities of garments, screen printing is a good option. If you need a more versatile process that can be used to print on a wider variety of materials, DTG printing is a better choice. And if you're looking for the highest quality prints on your garments, sublimation cut and sew is the best option.

No matter which method you choose, make sure to work with a reputable printing company that has experience in garment printing. This will ensure that you get high-quality prints that will last for years to come.

CHAPTER: 19

POP UP SHOPS: A POWERFUL MARKETING STRATEGY FOR YOUR BRAND

Pop up shops are temporary retail spaces that offer a unique and memorable shopping experience for customers. They can be set up anywhere, from vacant storefronts to festivals, malls, parks, or even online. Pop up shops are a great way to showcase your brand, test new products, generate buzz, and increase sales.

But how do you make the most of your pop up shop? How do you attract and engage your target audience? How do you measure the success of your pop up shop? And how do you use your social media platforms to promote your pop up shop and build a loyal fan base?

In this chapter, we will answer these questions and more. We will explore the benefits of pop up shops, the steps to plan and launch a successful pop up shop, and the best practices to use social media to market your pop up shop and your brand.

Why Pop Up Shops?

Pop up shops have many advantages for both brands and customers. Here are some of the benefits of pop up shops:

- **Create a sense of urgency and exclusivity.** Pop up shops are limited in time and space, which creates a sense of scarcity and FOMO (fear of missing out) among customers. Customers are more likely to visit your pop up shop and buy your products before they are gone.

- **Build brand awareness and loyalty.** Pop up shops allow you to showcase your brand personality and values, tell your story, and connect with your customers on a deeper level. You can also offer exclusive deals, samples, giveaways, or rewards to your pop up shop visitors, which can increase customer satisfaction and loyalty.

- **Test new products or markets.** Pop up shops are a low-risk and cost-effective way to test new products, concepts, or locations before investing in a permanent store. You can get direct feedback from your customers, measure their demand and preferences, and adjust your strategy accordingly.

- **Increase sales and revenue.** Pop up shops can boost your sales and revenue by attracting new customers, increasing impulse purchases, upselling or cross-selling complementary products, or clearing out excess inventory. You can also use pop up shops to generate leads, collect email addresses, or drive traffic to your website or social media channels.

How to Plan and Launch a Successful Pop Up Shop

Pop up shops require careful planning and execution to achieve your goals and deliver a positive customer experience. Here are some steps to follow when planning and launching your pop up shop:

- **Define your goals and budget.** What are you trying to achieve with your pop up shop? Do you want to increase brand awareness, test new products, generate sales, or something else? How will you measure your success? How much are you willing to spend on your pop up shop? These questions will help you set clear and realistic goals and budget for your pop up shop.

- **Choose your location and format.** Where do you want to set up your pop up shop? What kind of space do you need? How long do you want to run your pop up shop? These questions will help you choose the best location and format for your pop up shop. You can use online platforms like Storefront or Peerspace to find and book suitable spaces for your pop up shop. You can also consider partnering with other brands or venues that share your target audience or values.

- **Design your pop up shop.** How do you want your pop up shop to look and feel? What kind of atmosphere do you want to create? How will you display your products? How will you attract customers' attention? These questions will help you design your pop up shop. You can use props, signage, lighting, music, or interactive elements to make your pop up shop stand out and reflect your brand identity. You can also hire professional designers or decorators to help you with this step.

- **Promote your pop up shop.** How will you let people know about your pop up shop? How will you generate interest and excitement among your target audience? How will you encourage them to visit your pop up shop and buy your products? These questions will help you promote your pop up shop. You can use various channels such as email marketing, social media marketing, influencer marketing, press releases, flyers, or word-of-mouth to spread the word about your pop up shop. You can also create a hashtag or a landing page for your pop up shop to track its performance and engagement.

Run your pop up shop.

How will you manage the operations of your pop up shop? How will you handle inventory, payments, customer service, or security? How will you create a memorable shopping experience for your customers? These questions will help you run your pop up shop smoothly and effectively. Here are some tips to follow when running your pop up shop:

- **Prepare everything in advance.** Make sure you have everything you need for your pop up shop, such as products, equipment, staff, permits, insurance, or contracts.

Check the condition and functionality of your space and equipment before opening your pop up shop. Have a backup plan in case something goes wrong or unexpected.

- **Train your staff.** Make sure your staff are well-trained and informed about your brand, products, and goals. They should be friendly, helpful, and professional when interacting with customers. They should also be able to handle any issues or complaints that may arise during your pop up shop.
- **Offer multiple payment options.** Make it easy and convenient for your customers to pay for your products. You can use mobile payment systems such as Square or PayPal to accept credit cards, debit cards, or digital wallets. You can also offer cash payments, gift cards, or loyalty programs to increase customer satisfaction and retention.
- **Collect feedback and data.** Use your pop up shop as an opportunity to collect feedback and data from your customers. You can use surveys, polls, reviews, or social media posts to gather customer opinions and preferences. You can also use analytics tools such as Google Analytics or Shopify to track your sales, traffic, conversions, or referrals. This will help you measure the performance and impact of your pop up shop and improve your future strategies.
- **Create a memorable experience.** Make your pop up shop more than just a place to buy products. Make it an experience that your customers will remember and share with others. You can use storytelling, personalization,

gamification, or entertainment to engage your customers and make them feel special. You can also offer freebies, samples, discounts, or contests to reward your customers and increase their loyalty.

How to Use Social Media to Market Your Pop Up Shop and Your Brand

Social media is a powerful tool to market your pop up shop and your brand. It can help you reach a large and diverse audience, build relationships with your customers and influencers, generate buzz and awareness, and drive traffic and sales. Here are some ways to use social media to market your pop up shop and your brand:

- **Choose the right platforms.** Depending on your target audience and goals, you can choose the most suitable social media platforms for your pop up shop and brand. For example, you can use Instagram or Pinterest to showcase your products visually, Facebook or Twitter to share news and updates, YouTube or TikTok to create videos or live streams, or LinkedIn or Medium to share insights and expertise.

- **Create a content strategy.** Plan ahead what kind of content you want to create and share on your social media platforms. You can use a content calendar to schedule your posts and ensure consistency and quality. You can also use a content mix to balance different types of content such as educational, inspirational, promotional, or entertaining.

- **Engage with your audience.** Don't just post content on your social media platforms. Interact with your audience by responding to their comments,

Here is a possible chapter 19 that I wrote based on the information I found online. Please note that this is not legal advice and you should consult a lawyer before taking any action regarding your intellectual property.

CHAPTER 20
TRADEMARK AND COPYRIGHT

I f you have a brand or a business, you might wonder how to protect your name, logo, slogan, or any other distinctive element that identifies your products or services from others. You might also wonder how to protect your original works, such as books, videos, music, or software code, from being copied or used without your permission. In this chapter, we will explain the difference between trademark and copyright, two forms of intellectual property protection that can help you safeguard your brand and your creations.

What is a trademark?

A trademark is a word, phrase, design, or a combination of these that identifies your goods or services, distinguishes them from the goods or services of others, and indicates the source of your goods or services[2]. For example, Coca-Cola® is a trademark for soft drinks[2]. A trademark can also be a sound, color, shape, or smell that performs the same function[3]. For example, the NBC chimes are a trademark for broadcasting services[3].

A trademark can be registered with the U.S. Patent and Trademark Office (USPTO) to obtain nationwide legal protection[2]. A registered trademark gives you the exclusive right to use the mark in connection with your goods or services and to Prevent others from using a similar mark that might cause confusion among consumers[2]. A registered trademark also allows you to use the symbol ® next to your mark to indicate that it is registered[2].

However, registration is not mandatory to establish a trademark. You can also acquire trademark rights through common use of a mark in the course of business[2]. This means that if you use a distinctive mark to identify your goods or services in a certain geographic area, you can claim trademark rights in that area even without registration[2]. However, these rights are limited to that area and might not be enforceable against others who register or use the same or similar mark elsewhere[2]. To indicate that you claim trademark rights in an unregistered mark, you can use the symbol ™ next to your mark[2].

What is a copyright?

A copyright is a form of intellectual property protection that covers original works and is generated automatically by the creation of those works[1]. Original works are artistic, literary, or intellectually created works, such as novels, music, movies, software code, photographs, and paintings that are original and exist in a tangible medium[2]. For example, the song lyrics to "Let It Go" from "Frozen" are an original work[2].

A copyright gives you the exclusive right to reproduce, distribute, and perform or display the created work, and to prevent others from copying or exploiting the creation without your permission[2]. You can also grant permission to others to use your work by licensing or assigning your rights[2].

Although registration is not required to obtain copyright protection, it is highly recommended for several reasons. First, registration creates a public record of your claim of ownership and allows you to use the symbol © next to your work to indicate that it is protected[2]. Second, registration is necessary before you can sue someone for infringement and claim statutory damages and attorney's fees[2]. Third, registration can help prove that your work is original and that you created it first in case of a dispute[2].

What are the differences between trademark and copyright?

As you can see, trademark and copyright are both forms of intellectual property protection but they protect different types of assets and have different registration requirements. Here are some of the main differences:

- **Subject matter** : Trademark protects words, phrases, symbols, and designs used to identify and distinguish goods and services in the marketplace[4]. Copyright protects artistic, literary, or intellectually created works that are original and exist in a tangible medium[2].

- **Registration :** Trademark registration is optional but provides nationwide legal protection and exclusive rights to use the mark[2]. Copyright registration is optional but provides public record of ownership and enables legal action against infringement[2].

- **Duration :** Trademark rights last as long as the mark is used in commerce and maintained properly by filing periodic renewals with the USPTO[2]. Copyright rights last for the life of the author plus 70 years for individual works or 95 years from publication or 120

1. Trademark, patent, or copyright | USPTO. https://www.uspto.gov/trademarks/basics/trademark-patent-copyright.

2. Trademarks vs. copyrights: Which one is right for you?. https://www.legalzoom.com/articles/trademarks-vs-copyrights-which-one-is-right-for-you.

3. Copyright vs. Trademark: What's the Difference? – NerdWallet. https://www.nerdwallet.com/article/small-business/trademark-vs-copyright.

4. Trademarks vs Copyrights The 4 Important Differences Between. https://carsonpatents.com/trademarks-vs-copyrights/.

5. What is the difference between trademark and copyright?. https://www.lawbite.co.uk/resources/blog/what-is-the-difference-between-trademark-and-copyright.

Years from creation for works made for hire.

- **Symbol** : Trademark uses the symbols ® for registered marks and ™ for unregistered marks. Copyright uses the symbol © for registered or unregistered works.

How to use trademark and copyright for your brand?

If you have a brand or a business, you might want to use both trademark and copyright to protect your different aspects of your intellectual property. For example:

- You can use trademark to protect your brand name, logo, slogan, or any other distinctive element that identifies your products or services from others. This can help you build your reputation, prevent consumer confusion, and stop competitors from copying or misusing your brand identity.
- You can use copyright to protect your original works, such as books, videos, music, or software code, that you create for your business or as part of your products or services. This can help you control how your works are used, distributed, and monetized, and stop others from infringing on your creative rights.

To use trademark and copyright effectively, you should follow these steps:

- Conduct a search to make sure that your mark or work is not already registered or used by someone else in a similar way. You can use the USPTO's online databases for trademarks and copyrights, as well as other online sources, such as Google, Amazon, or social media platforms.
- Apply for registration with the USPTO if you want to obtain the maximum legal protection and benefits for your mark or work. You can use the USPTO's online application system or hire a lawyer to assist you with the process.
- Use the appropriate symbols next to your mark or work to indicate that it is protected and that you claim ownership of it. You can also include a notice with your contact information and terms of use to inform others of your rights and how they can obtain permission to use your mark or work.
- Monitor and enforce your rights by keeping track of how your mark or work is used in the marketplace and taking action against any unauthorized or infringing use. You can send a cease and desist letter, file a complaint with the USPTO, or sue in federal court if necessary.

CONCLUSION

I n this chapter, we have explained the difference between trademark and copyright, two forms of intellectual property protection that can help you safeguard your brand and your creations. We have also discussed how to use them effectively for your business. By understanding and applying these concepts, you can protect your intellectual property rights and prevent others from exploiting them without your permission.

BONUS CHAPTER

CHAPTER 21

HOW TO DO A DROP OR LAUNCH FOR A PRODUCT FOR YOUR STREETWEAR BRAND

I n the world of streetwear, a drop is a limited-edition release of new products. Drops are often used to create hype and excitement around a brand, and they can be a great way to boost sales.

If you're thinking about doing a drop for your streetwear brand, there are a few things you need to do to make sure it's a success.

1. **Plan your drop carefully.** The first step is to plan your drop carefully. This includes deciding on a date, time, and location for the drop. You'll also need to decide how many products you'll be releasing, and how much you'll charge for them.

2. **Create hype and excitement.** Once you have your plans in place, it's time to start creating hype and excitement around your drop. This can be done through social media, email marketing, and other channels. You can also partner with influencers to promote your drop.

3. **Make it easy to buy.** When it comes time for your drop, you need to make it easy for people to buy your products. This means having a well-designed website or app that can handle a high volume of traffic. You should also make sure your checkout process is simple and straightforward.

4. **Provide excellent customer service.** Even if you do everything else right, your drop can still be a failure if you don't provide excellent customer service. This means being responsive to customer inquiries, and resolving any issues quickly and efficiently.

By following these tips, you can increase your chances of success when you do a drop for your streetwear brand.

Here are some additional tips for a successful streetwear drop:

- **Create a sense of urgency.** Let your customers know that the products are limited-edition and that they won't be available for long. This will create a sense of urgency and encourage people to buy now.

- **Offer exclusive discounts or promotions.** This is a great way to incentivize people to buy your products during the drop. You can offer discounts, free shipping, or other special offers.

- **Partner with influencers.** Influencers can help you spread the word about your drop and generate excitement among your target audience. Reach out to influencers who have a large following of people who are interested in streetwear.

- **Run contests and giveaways.** This is a fun and engaging way to promote your drop and generate excitement among your customers. You can give away free products, gift cards, or other prizes.
- **Use social media.** Social media is a powerful tool for promoting your drop. Use social media to share photos and videos of your products, and to create hype and excitement around the drop.
- **Be prepared for high demand.** When you do a drop, it's important to be prepared for high demand. This means having enough products in stock, and having a well-designed website or app that can handle a lot of traffic.
- **Provide excellent customer service.** No matter how well you plan, there's always a chance that something will go wrong during your drop. That's why it's important to provide excellent customer service. Be responsive to customer inquiries, and resolve any issues quickly and efficiently.

By following these tips, you can increase your chances of success when you do a drop for your streetwear brand.

So, you're ready to start your own streetwear brand? Congratulations! This is an exciting time, but it's also a lot of work. But don't worry, you've got this.

I hope this book has given you the tools and knowledge you need to get started. Remember, the most important thing is to stay true to yourself and your vision. If you do that, you'll be well on your way to success.

Now go out there and make your mark on the world!"